BATTLE OF BRITAIN

by

Wallace B. Black
and
Jean F. Blashfield

CRESTWOOD HOUSE
New York

Collier Macmillan Canada
Toronto

Maxwell Macmillan International Publishing Group
New York Oxford Singapore Sydney

Library of Congress Cataloging-in-Publication Data

Black, Wallace B.
    Battle of Britain / by Wallace B. Black and Jean F. Blashfield. – 1st ed.
        p.   cm. – (World War II 50th anniversary series)
    Summary: Describes the three-month German bombing of Great Britain
in 1940 by the Luftwaffe, the errors made by the Germans, and the courage
of the British fliers and the public.
    ISBN 0-89686-553-3
    1. Britain, Battle of, 1940 – Juvenile literature. [1. Britain, Battle of.
2. World War, 1939-1945 – Great Britain.] I. Blashfield, Jean F.
II. Title. III. Series: Black, Wallace B. World War II 50th anniversary series.
D756.5.B7B56 1991
940.54'211 – dc20

                                                90-46579
                                                    CIP
                                                      AC

Created and produced by B & B Publishing, Inc.

Picture Credits

*Imperial War Museum - pages 7, 13, 17, 19, 21, 23, 29, 32, 34, 35, 36, 37, 42, 44 (center right),
    45 (center left, bottom)*
National Archives - pages 3, 4, 6, 8, 9, 10, 11, 14, 15, 18, 24, 25, 27, 30, 38, 40, 41
*United States Air Force - pages 26, 28, 33, 44 (top, center left, bottom),
    45 (top, center right)*
Steve Sullivan - Map - page 22

**CRESTWOOD
HOUSE**
    Macmillan Publishing Company
    866 Third Avenue
    New York, NY 10022
    Collier Macmillan Canada, Inc.
    1200 Eglinton Avenue East
    Suite 200
    Don Mills, Ontario M3C 3N1

Printed in the United States of America

First Edition

10 9 8 7 6 5 4 3 2 1

CONTENTS

Chapter 1

GREAT BRITAIN STANDS ALONE

It was July 1940. France and the other Allied nations had surrendered. The British people faced the German military might all alone.

Great Britain was hard at work rebuilding its battered armed forces. It was led by Prime Minister Winston Churchill. He encouraged his fellow countrymen to believe in victory. They waited for Adolf Hitler, the leader of Germany, to give the order for his army to invade the British Isles. But first the German air force would have to conquer the air. And the pilots of the Royal Air Force were not going to let that happen!

Despite reminders of impending war —like the barrage balloon meant to entangle enemy aircraft—the British carry on as usual.

The War in Europe

German planes and tanks attacked Poland on September 1, 1939. They conquered the country in just a few weeks. It was the world's first blitzkrieg, or "lightning war." Because Great Britain and France had sworn to defend Poland, both countries declared war on Germany. They quickly sent their armies to the border between France and Germany.

The troops waited, ready to fight. But nothing more happened for six months. People called that period the Phony War.

Then suddenly, Hitler struck again. In April 1940 Norway and Denmark fell to Germany. With hardly a pause—and no warning—German troops attacked Holland, Belgium and Luxembourg. These three countries surrendered within just a few weeks.

Rescue from the Beaches

France and Great Britain were unable to stop the German advances. The Germans used their blitzkrieg attack again. They drove quickly through Holland and Belgium and into France. The Dutch and Belgian armies were quickly defeated. The French and British armies suffered one defeat after another. They were driven north and west until their backs were against the English Channel.

More than 500,000 British and Frénch soldiers were trapped on the beaches near Dunkirk in France. Rapidly advancing German troops attacked from all sides. Panzer divisions came with their heavy tanks, motorized big guns and troop carriers. The mighty Luftwaffe (German air force) controlled the skies.

In desperation, Winston Churchill ordered Operation Dynamo. This called for the Royal Navy to rescue the troops trapped at Dunkirk. Huge numbers of vessels were pressed into service. Hundreds of privately owned motorboats, yachts and fishing boats were used.

Officers of the German Luftwaffe study the English Channel in preparation for war.

Day and night from May 25 to June 4, 1940, these small craft sailed to the beaches of Dunkirk. Hundreds of civilian volunteers put their own lives in danger to save the British and French troops. They carried 330,000 exhausted, wounded and defeated soldiers across the English Channel. There they would be safe on the shores of England. The British air force flew cover, trying to protect the ships and soldiers from Luftwaffe bombers.

The remaining French and British troops in France continued to fight. Paris, the capital, soon fell to the Germans. Seeing that the battle was hopeless, 200,000 British and French troops retreated across the channel to England. On June 21, 1940, the French government surrendered. France fell to the Germans just nine months after World War II began.

Britain's Last Chance

The Germans now looked hungrily across the English Channel toward Great Britain.

The British Isles were protected by the channel, a badly battered Royal Air Force and the Royal Navy. The armed forces were battle-weary and poorly armed. Help from

Captured British and French soldiers at Dunkirk

7

A victorious Hitler is hailed by the German people.

Australia and Canada was thousands of miles away. The civilian population lived in fear of invasion. The country was not ready for all-out war. For the moment, Britain seemed helpless.

Hitler thought that Great Britain would gladly ask for peace. He made fiery speeches to the German people and to the entire world. He praised the Germans for their victories. He asked that the British consider a peaceful end to the war. He thought that Germany and Great Britain could share the world and rule it together.

But Prime Minister Winston Churchill refused to listen to Hitler. He knew that the British people would not let Hitler keep the countries he had stolen. And he knew that the British would fight any attempted invasion. He spoke for most of the people of England, Scotland, Wales and Northern Ireland when he said:

". . .We shall defend our island, whatever the cost may be, we shall fight on the beaches, we shall fight on the landing grounds, we shall fight in the fields and in the streets, we shall fight in the hills; we shall never surrender."

Chapter 2

THE SEA LION AND THE EAGLE

Air-raid sirens screamed in the night! The roar of attacking planes and the thunder of exploding bombs echoed across England's shores.

It was just past midnight on the night of June 5, 1940. A small flight of German bombers crossed the English Channel. They attacked military targets in southeast England. Only the night before, the last of the British troops had been rescued from the beaches of France. The surrender of France was just a few days away. A German victory in Europe was certain.

When the war had first started nine months before, the British people had feared attack from the air. But it had not come. First, all action had stopped during the Phony War. Then the Luftwaffe had been too busy helping the German panzers capture the countries of western Europe.

British anti-aircraft crews rush to their guns to fight off approaching German bombers.

But now the Germans had reached the English Channel. The British people knew that if they didn't ask for peace, they would be invaded by German forces. The only democracy left in Europe was Britain.

England prepared for air raids, invasion and full-scale war. Then Adolf Hilter made a serious mistake. He thought the British people would ask for peace. After all, they had given him his way when he marched into Austria and Czechoslovakia and took over those countries. Surely the British did not want all-out war. He didn't need to waste men and aircraft by attacking the British Isles.

Hitler's generals were amazed. Most of them wanted to attack immediately. They were certain that if the British had time to recover and prepare, Germany would have a difficult time beating them.

The British built special defense systems along the English Channel. This floating "sea fort" is sliding off its barge into position.

The British test one of many defense tactics. Oil burns along the beaches to keep German craft from landing.

Germany Plans for Invasion

Just in case Britain did not give up, Hitler had plans for German troops to invade the British Isles and quickly take them over. His plan for the invasion had the code name Operation Sea Lion.

Two basic plans were considered for Operation Sea Lion. The first called for invasion from France across the narrow Strait of Dover. Dover is only about 20 miles across the channel from France. Surprise attacks by paratroops and other airborne units would come first. They would attack and capture key British airfields and seaports. Then additional troops could be landed by both sea and air. These troops would secure a larger coastal area for landing more troops and equipment.

A second plan called for a longer sea crossing from bases in Holland. This plan also called for massive airborne attacks. Landings at major ports northeast of London would be made by a huge invasion fleet carrying troops.

Most of the German leaders thought that the invasion would be easy, whichever route they took. They thought it would be no harder to move a quarter of a million troops across the channel than across a river.

But both plans had the same problems. For either invasion plan to succeed, both the Royal Air Force and coastal defenses had to be destroyed. In addition, the Royal Navy had to be kept away from the seaborne invasion forces.

Getting rid of these problems was the task of another German plan—Eagle. First, Eagle called for bombers and torpedo-planes from the German Luftwaffe to destroy all ships that sailed in the English Channel. That would force the Royal Navy to stay out of the channel. Luftwaffe fighter planes would destroy RAF planes as they tried to protect the navy. Then the German army, under the protection of the Luftwaffe, would launch Operation Sea Lion, the invasion of the British Isles.

Operation Eagle was under the command of Reichsmarschall Hermann Goering, head of the Luftwaffe. He controlled a mighty air force of over 4,000 aircraft. He was certain that his pilots could sweep the shattered Royal Air Force from the skies.

Hitler was sure that the combined forces of Eagle and Sea Lion would let him succeed in taking over Great Britain. The British Isles had not been successfully invaded by a foreign army for almost 1,000 years. But Hitler thought he could do it.

Hitler might have succeeded if he had not delayed. German troops could have followed the defeated British army across the channel immediately after it was rescued from Dunkirk. But Hitler stopped further aerial attacks on Great Britain and immediate invasion plans. The German army was busy conquering France and enjoying the victory celebrations that followed. This waiting period gave the British people a month to lick their wounds and prepare to defend their homeland.

Hermann Goering (left) boasted that his Luftwaffe would "sweep the RAF from the skies." The RAF proved him wrong.

New Hurricane fighter aircraft being readied for combat

Britain Builds Defenses

British factories worked 24 hours a day to turn out new aircraft and guns. In the month after Dunkirk, more than 300 new fighter aircraft were built. Shiploads of guns and ammunition bought from the United States arrived daily. Radar stations were quickly built so that they could give warning of approaching German aircraft. Radar was a new, secret technique that used radio waves to find the location and height of enemy aircraft.

Civilians were busy too. Gas masks were distributed to all of them because Germany had used poison gas in World War I. Young children were sent to the country, away from cities that might be bombed. People too young or too old to serve in the military formed the Home Guard. This group would help protect the homeland against an invading force.

On June 18, 1940, Churchill spoke to his people, thanking them for what they were doing and what they still had to do. He said:

"The Battle of Britain is about to begin. . . . Let us therefore brace ourselves to our duties, and so bear ourselves that if the British Empire and its Commonwealth last for a thousand years, men will still say: 'This was their finest hour.'"

The Channel Islands are small British islands just off the coast of France. They could not be protected. So from June 19 to 24, more than 20,000 British citizens from the islands of Jersey, Guernsey and Sark were evacuated to Great Britain. Some residents decided to stay. The Germans invaded the islands on June 30 and stayed for more than four years.

Sometimes German airplanes ventured over Great Britain. On July 6, a lone intruder dropped bombs on a British air base, killing two Canadians. No one had stopped the single aircraft because the British were trying to keep Germany from knowing just how good their air defenses were.

British children leaving their homes and families to be safe from the bombings in London. They were sent to the countryside for the duration of the war.

Chapter 3

THE CHANNEL BATTLE
July 10 – August 12

It was just after noon on July 10, 1940, a beautiful summer day. A convoy of British supply ships was sailing down the English Channel from Dover. A British radar station picked up radio signals bouncing off a large flight of airplanes, perhaps 120 or more. German Dornier Do 17 bombers (called "flying pencils"), protected by Messerschmitt Me 109 and Me 110 fighters, were about to attack the defenseless convoy.

But British radar operators were alert. Told of the approaching German aircraft, the RAF Ground Control alerted Fighter Command. RAF squadrons of Hurricanes and Spitfires quickly took to the air. The RAF fighter aircraft, diving out of the sun, attacked the giant formations of German bombers and their fighter escorts. They took them completely by surprise.

The British fighters were led by skilled pilots, Squadron Leaders "Spider" Malan and Doug Bader. They dove on the escorting German fighters. Dogfights, battles between two opposing aircraft, filled the sky. These violent encounters lasted only about 15 minutes. Nine Luftwaffe aircraft were shot down, while only two British fighters were lost. The attackers fled back to their bases in France. Only one vessel of the convoy was sunk.

Hitler and his commanders were still arguing about how and when to invade England. But Reichsmarschall Hermann Goering's pilots had already begun the Battle of Britain.

A formation of Heinkel He 111 bombers on a raid over England. The He 111s flew many raids in the Battle of Britain.

Eagle Is Surprised

On July 10 the British started to show the Germans that they had a fight on their hands. Goering was not going to find it easy to keep his promise to "sweep the RAF from the skies." The Luftwaffe pilots were surprised at the strength and speed of the defending British aircraft.

Within a short time, the Luftwaffe realized that British radar stations quickly knew just when and where they would attack. Although greatly outnumbered, the RAF Hurricanes and Spitfires were always in the air and ready for battle when the German aircraft arrived.

General Wolfram von Richthofen commanded a group of Ju 87 Stuka dive-bombers. These planes had had great success in Poland and in the battle for France. The pilots expected to get the same results against England. On July 11 a dozen of Richthofen's Stukas, with Me 109 fighters flying cover, attacked a convoy.

Ju 87 Stuka dive-bombers preparing to attack

RAF Hurricane fighters taking off to intercept German attackers

Guided by radar, Hurricanes and Spitfires dove on the attackers. Although several RAF fighters were destroyed, the attacking force was scattered. Many Stukas were lost. Soon after, Goering took the Stukas out of the Battle of Britain. They were no match for the high-speed British fighters.

The air battles over the English Channel continued. Both sides lost aircraft and pilots. On July 12 a flight of three RAF Hurricane fighters shot down or damaged at least four Do 17 bombers. A few days later British ace "Spider" Malan and his squadron tangled with German ace Werner Molder's Me 109 squadron. A half-dozen Me 109s went down in flames or were damaged. The bombers they were protecting turned back.

Hitler was not concerned. He was certain that his Luftwaffe pilots would soon take control of the channel. On July 16 he sent out secret orders to his generals to prepare for Operation Sea Lion. They would invade England in September!

Building New Airplanes

Meanwhile, the RAF was building up its fighter squadrons. They had been left after Dunkirk with only about 500 fighter aircraft. But by early July they had over 800 aircraft. However, many planes needed repair. Air Chief Marshal Sir Hugh Dowding was in charge of Fighter Command. He was trying to build his fighter force for the major battles he knew would come.

The Battle of Britain was fought not only in the air. It was also fought in the factories. Working 24 hours a day, people in British aircraft factories were turning out an average of 400 new fighters a month.

The Luftwaffe continued its channel warfare against convoys and coastal defenses. But it also began to strike inland. Airfields, radar stations and anti-aircraft batteries (large guns with the power to shoot down airplanes) became targets.

Pilot Losses

There were not enough trained RAF pilots to replace the ones shot down. The experienced pilots fought carefully. They tried not to fight when outnumbered. They often attacked the invaders only after they were about to reach their targets. Each day the pilots learned more about aerial combat. And each day brought more pilots out of training and ready for action.

Toward the end of July the Luftwaffe increased its aerial attacks. Still learning the skills of aerial combat, the RAF lost over 100 aircraft during the fierce fighting. Sometimes the pilots were able to parachute safely to the ground. Sometimes they died when their planes went down in flames. Sometimes they crashed into the channel and had to be rescued.

Aerial battles over the channel and coastal defenses of England became more furious. English convoys were attacked daily. Sometimes many ships were lost because their fighter protection did not arrive soon enough. However, the courageous pilots of the Hurricanes and Spitfires of Fighter Command helped most coastal shipping get through.

The Luftwaffe was not winning the channel battle. Hitler ordered Goering to increase the number of attacks the Luftwaffe flew each day. Operation Sea Lion was almost ready to be launched. But Goering had not yet kept his promise to clear the English Channel and the skies of England.

Starting in mid-July, landing barges, ships and craft of every description were being readied along the coast of France. Huge quantities of supplies and equipment were rushed from Germany to the French coast. Troops were trained for both seaborne and airborne invasions.

But the big problem remained. Operation Eagle still had to clear the skies over the English Channel.

German Major Adolf Galland (left) *and British Squadron Leader Douglas Bader were both aces and great officers. At another time and in another place, they probably would have been good friends. By the end of the war, Bader had lost both of his legs but was still flying.*

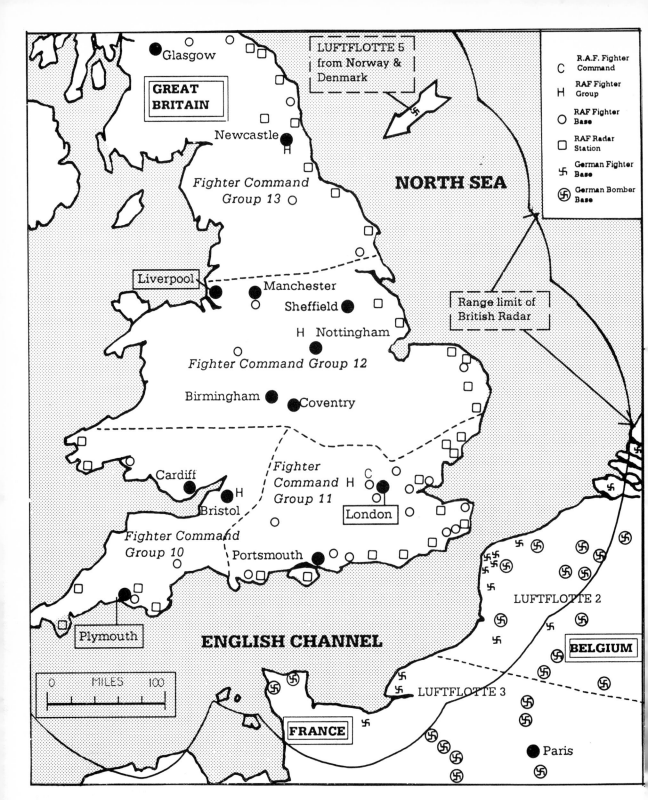

LUFTFLOTTE 5
from Norway &
Denmark

GREAT
BRITAIN

Glasgow

Newcastle

*Fighter Command
Group 13*

NORTH SEA

R.A.F. Fighter
Command

RAF Fighter
Group

RAF Fighter
Base

RAF Radar
Station

German Fighter
Base

German Bomber
Base

Liverpool

Manchester

Sheffield

Nottingham

Fighter Command Group 12

Range limit of
British Radar

Birmingham

Coventry

Cardiff

*Fighter
Command
Group 11*

London

Bristol

*Fighter Command
Group 10*

Portsmouth

LUFTFLOTTE 2

BELGIUM

Plymouth

ENGLISH CHANNEL

LUFTFLOTTE 3

0   MILES   100

FRANCE

Paris

22

Chapter 4

OPPOSING AIR FORCES

Both France and Great Britain had begun building their air forces in the years before the war. Even so, compared to the German Luftwaffe, the Allies were poorly prepared.

In the fall of 1939, Great Britain had 1,900 active aircraft, France about 1,000. Poland had only 500. Many of these aircraft were out-of-date. The RAF had only about 100,000 men, including pilots and ground crews. Only a few had flown in combat and that had been in World War I.

By the following June, the entire French and Polish air forces had been destroyed. The RAF had only about 500 Hurricanes and Spitfires and a few bombers left. The RAF had fought bravely during the air battles over France, but its numbers were no match for the Luftwaffe.

RAF pilots run toward their aircraft after being warned of approaching enemy planes.

Taken from a German aircraft,
this dramatic picture shows an
RAF Spitfire breaking away
after attacking a German Do 17
(flying pencil) bomber.

By comparison, the Germans had over 4,000 aircraft and an air force of 500,000 men. During its great victories leading up to the fall of France, the Luftwaffe had gained valuable experience. Finally, the Germans occupied captured French, Dutch and Belgian airfields along the English Channel. They were more than ready for the Battle of Britain.

The Luftwaffe

Hermann Goering was the commander in chief of the Luftwaffe. He had been a famous pilot and a German war hero in World War I. Even more important to Hitler, Goering was a high-ranking member of the Nazi party. He believed that his Luftwaffe would easily defeat the Royal Air Force in the coming battle. After all, German pilots had proved their superior tactics and fighting ability in Spain and in the conquests of Poland, Holland, Belgium and France.

Air attacks on Great Britain began in early July 1940. The Luftwaffe had assigned these air raids to three divisions called *Luftflottes*, which means "air fleets."

A formation of Heinkel He 111 bombers en route to a target in England

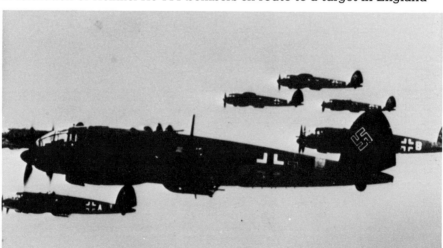

An artist's drawing of Messerschmitt Me 109s providing fighter protection as German bombers attack

A Junkers Ju 87 Stuka could dive-bomb with great accuracy. But it could not match the RAF's Hurricanes and Spitfires for speed.

Luftflotte 2 was commanded by General Albert Kesselring and Luftflotte 3 by General Hugo Sperrle. They were stationed in Holland, Belgium and France, just a few air miles from their targets in England. Luftflotte 5, commanded by General Hans-Sturgen Stumpff, was stationed in Denmark and Norway.

All three commanders were experienced and brilliant officers. Kesselring's and Sperrle's divisions were the largest. They had the task of destroying the Royal Air Force. They also attacked Allied shipping and naval forces in the English Channel.

The three air fleets combined had over 2,800 bomber and fighter aircraft, with several thousand more in reserve. Their air and ground crews had already experienced combat with great success.

They also had such experienced leaders as General Wolfram von Richthofen, cousin of the "Red Baron" of World War I fame. Another ace, Adolf Galland, had helped to organize the Luftwaffe. He personally attracted many excellent pilots to the Nazi air force.

Against this vast air force, the British had fewer than 500 ready fighters and few experienced pilots.

The Royal Air Force

What the RAF lacked in numbers of both pilots and aircraft it made up for in leadership. It also possessed a few highly skilled pilots who had survived the air battles over France. Both the Hurricanes and Spitfires of the RAF were excellent fighter aircraft.

RAF Fighter Command was headed by Sir Hugh Dowding. More than any other individual, he was responsible for the success of the RAF in the Battle of Britain.

With so few aircraft and even fewer experienced pilots, the RAF was fighting an uphill battle. But new pilots and new aircraft joined the squadrons daily. During July daily combat gave the young pilots the experience they needed. But many died as their comrades learned to fight the well-trained and well-equipped Luftwaffe.

(Left) *Sir Hugh Dowding provided superb leadership throughout the Battle of Britain.*

(Below) *Squadron Leader Stanford Tuck sitting in his Hurricane fighter. Tuck was a leading RAF ace. The Nazi symbols on his aircraft indicate that he had already shot down 23 German aircraft.*

Radar was called the "silent weapon" of World War II. More than 50 radar stations along the English Channel and North Sea alerted the British to approaching enemy aircraft.

Four RAF groups of Fighter Command protected the British Isles from northern Scotland to the southern tip of England. They were ready day and night to meet attacking Luftwaffe squadrons.

Radar: The RAF's "Silent Helper"

As the Battle of Britain was starting, the German attackers often found British fighters already aloft and ready to fight. They could not understand how the British always seemed to know they were coming. But they soon found the reason why. Radar!

Radar stands for RAdio Detection And Ranging. This electronic device had been researched in a number of countries before the war. Germany was aware of its value but had planned to use it only at sea. Great Britain was the first to put it to good use in identifying approaching aircraft.

Radar stations are equipped with fixed or rotating antennas. They send out radio waves in a chosen direction. When the radio waves hit a solid object, they bounce back to a receiving station. Operators on the ground watch a screen that shows the continuous stream of bounced-back signals as "blips" of light. The operators are then able to tell the distance, the direction, the altitude and the speed of approaching aircraft.

The British had built radar stations all along their coasts in the years before the war. But their accuracy was a carefully guarded secret. Expert technicians at the British radar stations knew almost at once when Luftwaffe squadrons took off from France. As their skills developed, the operators could tell enough about the approaching aircraft to let the right squadrons be warned and ready.

The RAF Fighter Command Ground Control System had more than 50 radar transmitting and receiving towers stationed all along the English Channel. Radar operators would immediately report any radar sightings of approaching German aircraft.

Fighter Command and Control System

Radar stations and the 30,000 members of the Royal Observer Corps spotted attacking aircraft. The Observer Corps was controlled by the military. However, it was made up mostly of civilians who were too old or physically unable to serve on active duty.

When a radar operator or an observer sighted enemy aircraft approaching, he telephoned or radioed the information to the Fighter Command Ground Control. The controllers there plotted the location and movement of the approaching enemy on huge maps. As soon as sightings and direction of attack were definite, the information would be called in to Fighter Command Headquarters.

At headquarters, Dowding and his staff would then call one of the Fighter Command Groups. At air bases where fighter squadrons were stationed, a siren would blast. The eager flight crews would run to their airplanes. Within minutes of a report of an approaching enemy force, Hurricanes and Spitfires would be in the air to meet the attackers.

Once the war got under way, radar and ground control stations were staffed mainly by members of the Women's Auxiliary Air Force. The WAAF and the Royal Observer

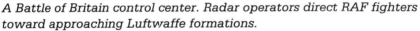

A Battle of Britain control center. Radar operators direct RAF fighters toward approaching Luftwaffe formations.

First line of defense during the Battle of Britain. Spitfire fighters, guided by radar, set out to intercept German aircraft.

Corps had thousands of men and women on active duty. For 24 hours a day, they watched and listened at posts throughout England. They were always on the alert for the enemy.

Fighter Command Headquarters was notified of all sightings of enemy aircraft, whether they were made by radar or by ground observers. Defending squadrons were then ordered to "scramble"—to take off and intercept the attackers. As a result, Spitfire and Hurricane fighters were usually ready to attack before the German planes neared their targets. Anti-aircraft artillery units would also be alerted. The men and women who controlled the big guns would then be ready to fire at the enemy planes as they flew overhead.

Hundreds of barrage balloons were also put in place to trap low-flying attackers. These were large hydrogen-filled balloons that were raised and lowered by long cables. Balloons were placed near and around important ground targets, such as aircraft factories. Unsuspecting attackers would fly into the balloons or the cables and crash.

Without radar, the Observer Corps, and Fighter Command Ground Control, the British would have been defeated by the Germans. And democracy would have been lost in Europe.

Chapter 5

EAGLE ATTACK
August 13 – September 6

Preparations for Operation Sea Lion were going forward. The Luftwaffe needed a great victory. Its previous tactics had failed. The channel battle cost the Germans over 280 aircraft, while the British had lost only 150 fighters. A giant attack was necessary, one that would stop the fighters before they could get into the air. Goering called the plan Eagle Attack (*Adlerangriffe*). The goal was to destroy the enemy on the ground—before they could get into the air.

As smoke billows from earlier bomb blasts, two Dornier Do 217 bombers fly over an RAF airfield and neighboring factories.

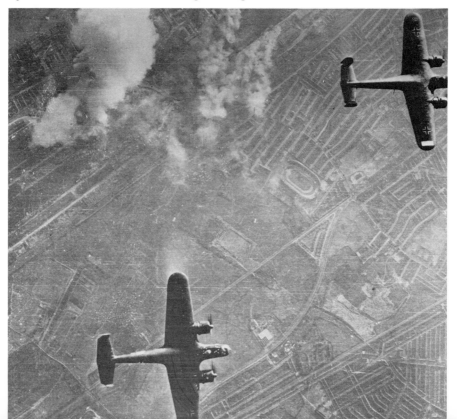

Trails formed by RAF and Luftwaffe planes dogfighting high above the British Isles

Scheduled to start on August 5, the first attack actually took place on August 13. That day was called *Adlertag,* or Eagle Day. Luftwaffe pilots flew 1,500 sorties (a mission by a single aircraft) against major targets along the southeast coast of England and inland. British pilots took to the air again and again and again. They fought to the point of exhaustion and beyond.

Both sides claimed large numbers of enemy destroyed. Goering and his staff celebrated a great victory. But when the official count was in, they found that the Luftwaffe had lost 45 aircraft while the RAF had lost only 13. Goering was furious.

Radar had supplied advance reports of the coming attacks, but something else had given the British an additional advantage. The British had broken a code used by the Germans in radioing messages. Because of that, RAF Fighter Command had had advance information about the plans for Eagle Day.

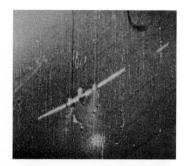

The Eagle Continues

Eagle Attack continued. The Luftwaffe struck in huge numbers. They hit seaports as well as air bases, factories and other targets far inland. On August 15 the Germans flew the largest number of missions in the Battle of Britain up to that time—almost 1,800 sorties! The air battles stretched over a 500-mile-wide area. That day the Germans lost about 75 bombers and fighters, and the RAF had only 35 of its planes shot down.

During the first week of Eagle Attack, RAF pilots made more than 190 confirmed "kills" of German aircraft. Many pilots became aces that week. To become an ace, a pilot had to shoot down five aircraft. Each one had to be confirmed. That meant that another person had seen the action or the pilot parachuting out of his plane or that the wreckage of the aircraft was later found.

Most of the British kills were of the Ju 87 Stuka dive-bombers and the Me 110 two-place fighters. Goering ordered the Stukas withdrawn from further combat in Britain. He ordered the Me 110s used as bombers and night fighters only.

Goering had received false reports of huge losses by the RAF. He thought the RAF was down to around 300 ready aircraft. German victory seemed only days away. True, the RAF had suffered losses, but it actually still had over 700 Spitfires and Hurricanes ready for battle.

Photos taken by a gun camera mounted on an RAF fighter. Smoking and flaring tracer bullets are seen striking a Luftwaffe bomber.

As air battles rage nearby, RAF ground crewmen repair a Hawker Hurricane.

The real problem for the British was the shortage of pilots. Factories could turn out airplanes, but they could not make new pilots. Available air crew members were exhausted and unable to keep up with the demands of combat. Many brave young pilots were being killed daily, and hundreds more were wounded. Ground crews were suffering from continuous Luftwaffe attacks on airfields. But the few brave pilots and the men on the ground kept the Hurricanes and Spitfires flying against the Germans.

Nonstop Bombing!

At this point, the German commanders again decided to change tactics. Instead of engaging in aerial combat with fighter planes, they would send huge flights of bombers deep into industrial England. Their targets were to be not only RAF airfields but also aircraft factories, oil tanks, railway yards and other vital ground installations. Attacks were to be carried on nonstop, day and night!

This new phase of the battle took a terrible toll on both the RAF pilots and the planes they flew. And it also caused arguments among RAF commanders. They could not agree on how to stem the tide of increasing attacks and increasing losses. Airfields were being bombed so heavily that they could not be used.

Pilots and ground crews were becoming even more exhausted. Fighter pilots were flying five and six missions a day. Pilots who had never flown high-speed fighters were even borrowed from the Royal Navy. Even with all its problems, the RAF was still scoring heavily against the attackers. But how long could the British hold out?

Finally, on August 31, Luftwaffe bombing attacks had made most of the RAF air bases near the English coast unusable. Aircraft returning from missions often found their bases destroyed. Many experienced pilots and many aircraft were lost.

That was the worst day for Fighter Command. For the first time the RAF had lost more planes than it had destroyed. Hugh Dowding was bewildered about what he should do next.

Then suddenly German tactics changed again.

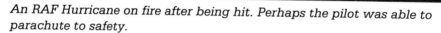

An RAF Hurricane on fire after being hit. Perhaps the pilot was able to parachute to safety.

Chapter 6

THE BLITZ
September 7 – 30

All during the months of July and August, Hitler had issued strict instructions not to bomb London. He thought that the Luftwaffe could win the Battle of Britain without causing civilian casualties or damaging the British capital. However, on the night of August 23, several Luftwaffe bomber aircraft went off course and accidentally dropped bombs on London. As Hitler feared, this enraged the British. To get even, the RAF bombed Berlin, the capital of Germany, two nights later.

By early September the Luftwaffe had destroyed many airfields and factories in daytime raids. It seemed as if the RAF would be defeated. It is likely that if the Luftwaffe had continued its daytime raids, it would have destroyed the Royal Air Force and won the war.

However, Hitler became angered by the bombing of Berlin and the loss of over 100 aircraft in one week. Once again, he decided to change tactics. He ordered day and night bombing raids on London and other major cities. The Blitz, as the British called the round-the-clock bombing of London, started on September 7.

London on Fire

Huge flights of Heinkel He 111, Junkers Ju 88, Messerschmitt Me 110 and Dornier Do 17 bombers swarmed over the cities. They dropped their loads of death and destruction. The damage in the crowded city of London was terrible. Thousands of houses and office buildings were destroyed. Thousands more were set on fire. Fire trucks

The Blitz begins! Stunned Londoners look for their possessions among the rubble.

could not get through the damaged streets to fight the blazes. Thousands of civilians died.

On the night of September 15 alone, over 1,000 bombers attacked. The Luftwaffe lost 56 planes. The British fought on. Night after night, the air-raid sirens would sound. Londoners would hurry into air-raid shelters, basements and subway train stations. Night after night, they emerged from bomb shelters to see if their homes had been destroyed, if their families and friends were alive. During the first weeks of the Blitz, over 2,000 Londoners died and more than 10,000 were wounded. Hundreds were buried in the burning and crumbling buildings, never to be found.

Strangely, these terrible bombings and the successes of the Luftwaffe over London actually helped the British. They became so angry that they worked harder than ever. They were even more determined not to give in to Hitler.

King George VI of England and his wife, Queen Elizabeth, survey bomb damage to Buckingham Palace.

With the bombing concentrated on London, aircraft factories elsewhere quickly got back into production. Airfields were repaired. Even the war-weary pilots of the RAF were able to rest. As the people of London suffered, the RAF and other British defenses were strengthened.

Invasion Canceled!

Hitler waited eagerly for reports that the British people were ready to give up.

But they didn't come. The determination of the British people had not been broken. Even worse for Hitler, the Luftwaffe was suffering severe losses.

Eagle Attack and the Blitz had failed to prepare the way for invasion. On September 17 Hitler officially postponed Operation Sea Lion. Eventually he completely canceled the planned invasion of the British Isles. But, of course, the British people did not know that.

Evidence of the success of the RAF. The wreckage of a Luftwaffe bomber lies in a British field.

The British had prevented the invasion of their homeland. But they could not prevent much of that homeland from being heavily bombed. The Luftwaffe kept up the bombings of major cities. These attacks, mostly at night, continued throughout the rest of 1940.

The terrible attack on the city of Coventry was the worst. It came without warning. Five hundred Heinkel He 111 bombers dropped over 500 tons of bombs on the night of November 14. The famous old Coventry Cathedral was ruined. More than 50,000 other buildings were blasted, and almost 400 people died that terrible night. Hitler had named the raid on Coventry Moonlight Sonata. It proved to be a tragic song for the British people.

Still they fought on. The death and destruction caused by the Blitz brought the people of the British Isles closer together. The armed forces were learning how to fight the enemy. Goering and his mighty Luftwaffe had failed to bring Churchill's government and the brave British people to their knees. Eagle had failed. Sea Lion never happened.

Disappointed, Hitler turned his attention away from Great Britain. He ordered his troops to advance into Russia. But no matter what conquests the Germans made from then on, they always knew that the British were busily rearming. Great Britain was determined to keep fighting. The Germans would continue bombing Britain, but the British would soon start heavy bombing of the Germans' own homeland. And at the end of 1941, the United States Air Force would join them.

So Few

The British people and the British armed forces had withstood the greatest aerial attack in history. All fought valiantly—the people in the streets, the workers in the factories, the WAAFs in aircraft control, the anti-aircraft and barrage balloon crews, the Home Guard. But especially the men of the Fighter Command of the Royal Air Force.

Hundreds of young pilots, barely out of their teens, took part. Fighting alongside the Englishmen were Canadians, Australians, men of the Polish and French air forces, and even American volunteers who formed the Eagle Squadron. All fought and many died to keep Hitler's armies from invading the British Isles.

Day after day and night after night, these brave young men climbed into their Spitfires and Hurricanes. They flew skyward to face death. Hundreds of the British Empire's finest youth fought, were terribly wounded, or died in the greatest aerial battle of all time. And they won.

In the immortal words of Winston Churchill, "Never in the field of human conflict was so much owed by so many to so few."

The brave young men of the Fighter Command of the Royal Air Force had withstood the fierce German attack. Eagle had failed and Operation Sea Lion had been canceled. The people of Great Britain would be forever grateful.

The Battle of Britain was over!

A Closer Look at . . .

AIRCRAFT OF THE LUFTWAFFE

The Messerschmitt Me 109 *(right)* was the best fighter aircraft of the early war years. A single-seat, low-wing monoplane, it was faster and more maneuverable than its RAF opponents. It was limited by very short range. It was armed with a combination of machine guns and 20 mm cannon.

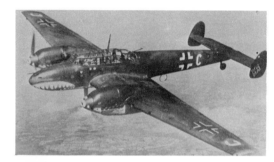

The Messerschmitt Me 110 *(left)* was originally intended for use as a daytime fighter and bomber. A twin-engine, low-wing monoplane, it carried a crew of two. During the Battle of Britain it was found to be slow and clumsy. So it was later used as a bomber and night fighter. It carried a variety of forward- and rear-firing guns as well as a bomb-load of 1,100 pounds.

The Junkers Ju 87 Stuka *(right)* was the first successful dive-bomber of World War II. A low-wing, single-engine monoplane, it carried a crew of two. It aimed its bomb-load by diving at a steep angle directly toward its target. It had loud sirens that screamed as it dove. It carried a bomb-load of up to 3,900 pounds and a variety of forward- and rear-firing guns.

The Junkers Ju 88 *(left)* was one of several twin-engine medium bombers used by the Luftwaffe. This low-winged monoplane carried a crew of four with a bomb-load of up to 5,500 pounds. It was equipped with a variety of fixed and flexible forward- and rear-firing machine guns.

AIRCRAFT OF THE RAF

The Supermarine Spitfire *(right)* was one of the great fighter aircraft of World War II. A single-seat, low-wing monoplane, it was very fast and maneuverable. It was armed with several machine guns or 20 mm cannon.

The Hawker Hurricane *(left),* though not as fast and maneuverable as the Spitfire, was credited with more victories in the early days of the war. Also a single-seat, low-wing monoplane, it was armed with up to 12 machine guns.

The Bristol Beaufighter *(right)* was a twin-engine monoplane with a crew of two. It was used during the Battle of Britain as a night fighter but could also be used as a daytime light bomber. It carried a bomb-load of 2,000 pounds and a combination of 10 forward-firing cannon and machine guns plus one flexible-mounted rear-firing machine gun.

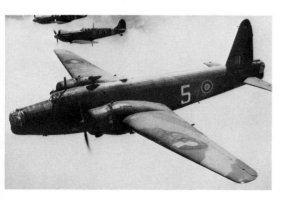

The Vickers-Armstrong Wellington *(left)* was one of the RAF's medium bombers. It could carry a bomb-load of 4,000 pounds and was one of the first bombers used against Germany. With a crew of six, it was equipped with forward- and rear-firing gun turrets as well as several flexible gun mounts.

GLOSSARY

ace A pilot who has successfully shot down five enemy aircraft.

Allies The nations that opposed Germany, Japan and Italy during WWII: Great Britain, the United States, the Soviet Union and France.

barrage balloons Large hydrogen-filled balloons raised in the air by cables. Used to defend ground targets from enemy aircraft.

blitzkrieg Means "lightning war" in German.

dogfight Aerial combat between individual fighter aircraft of opposing air forces.

Ground Control An air force unit that received information concerning approaching enemy aircraft and directed activities of its own air force against the attackers.

gun turrets Plastic-covered machine-gun mountings on aircraft, which can be controlled by a gunner to fire in several directions.

kill The successful shooting down of a single enemy aircraft.

low wing Referring to a monoplane (single-wing aircraft); the wing extends from the bottom of the body of the aircraft.

Luftwaffe The German air force before and during World War II.

monoplane An aircraft with one wing.

Nazi A member of the German National Socialist party, the political party developed by Hitler.

panzer A German tank. A "panzer unit" in the German army was equipped with tanks and other motorized and armored vehicles.

radar Radio equipment used to detect targets such as airplanes and determine their distance, speed and height. Short for RAdar Detection And Ranging.

Reichsmarschall The title assumed by Hermann Goering as chief of the German air force.

sortie One mission by a single aircraft against an enemy.

squadron A group of aircraft or ships in an air force or navy.

torpedo-planes Aircraft equipped to carry and launch torpedoes while in flight.

INDEX